E
7
A.

C000039134

Galatians

FREEDOM IN CHRIST

CWR

John Houghton

Published 2011 by CWR, Waverley Abbey House, Waverley Lane, Farnham, Surrey GU9 8EP, UK. Registered Charity No. 294387. Registered Limited Company No. 1990308.

See back of book for list of National Distributors.

Unless otherwise indicated, all Scripture references are from the Holy Bible: New International Version (NIV), copyright © 1973, 1978, 1984 by the International Bible Society.

Concept development, editing, design and production by CWR

Cover image: istock/Zakharchenko

Printed in England by Page Brothers

ISBN: 978-1-85345-648-0

Contents

Introduction

Paul's letter to the Galatians is the Magna Carta of religious freedom. It is a powerful and passionate rejection of all religions that depend on rule keeping, ritual and regulations for their efficacy. Salvation is by faith in Christ alone, without any additional help from us or anyone else. Faith in Christ makes us right with God, assures us of eternal life, incorporates us into the true people of God, and provides the only basis for a society that is both free and moral. Its message is clear, convincing and compassionate. Seldom has it been more needed than in our contemporary society.

Opinions differ over precisely who constituted Paul's original target audience. In 278 BC marauding Celtic tribes called Gauls reached Asia Minor (Turkey) and settled in the central heartlands. These restless warriors became known as Galatians. Rome eventually secured law and order and in 25 BC established an enlarged Roman province called Galatia that included some southern, non-Celtic parts of Asia Minor. Some think Paul wrote to the ethnic northern Galatians around AD 56–57; others that he addressed the churches that he had planted in the south of the province around AD 49. Most favour the latter, but it remains disputed.

What isn't in dispute is that the apostle Paul himself wrote this letter, and for very good reasons. His apostolic work in the region was being undermined by supposed believers known as Judaisers, or Jew-makers. These people said that Paul had short-changed them by not giving them the whole gospel. Furthermore, that his teaching came second-hand from Antioch rather than from Jerusalem. He wasn't even one of the original Twelve, and it was known that he had actually challenged Peter's authority!

The Galatian Christians were confused. Paul had blessed them with the gospel of Christ; the Holy Spirit worked miracles in their midst. But were they fully saved? Or could the work of Christ in their lives only be complete if they observed the Law of Moses as well? Some were already practising the Jewish feast days; it was likely that many would soon undergo circumcision. It was even suggested that because Paul had circumcised Timothy and not the Galatians, he was withholding something from them.

Paul had no illusions about the impact of this teaching. If being saved requires faith in Jesus, plus adherence to the Law of Moses, then the Christian faith is no more than a sect of Judaism. Since the Jews believed that keeping the Law of Moses was itself sufficient for peace with God, Christ's death was superfluous. Jesus died for nothing. Gentiles then have no hope unless they become Jews, but ironically, adopting the Law of Moses cannot save a Gentile any more than it can save a Jew.

The path of lawlessness cannot save, but nor can the way of legalism. We are justified by faith alone or we are not justified at all. Legalism and lawlessness are just two sides of the same coin – the works of the sinful nature. Faith in Christ sets us free to produce the fruit of the Spirit – the liberty to love which is the hallmark of the true people of God, and the highest moral order for a civilised society.

We tend to think of witchcraft in terms of stereotypical occult practices, but these Galatians were being deceived by a distortion of the truth. Such satanic activity is as old as the Garden of Eden. Jesus said, 'You will know the truth, and the truth will set you free' (John 8:32). May we find true freedom in Christ as we study this book.

WEEK 1

Good News and Bad News

Opening Icebreaker

Imagine this scenario: One of your children is diagnosed with Type 1 diabetes. The doctor prescribes insulin injections. One nurse gives, instead, an injection of tea; another gives an injection of insulin laced with strychnine. The third gives proper insulin. Discuss what should happen to the first two nurses.

Bible Readings

- Galatians 1:1–10
- 2 Corinthians 11:1–6, 13–15
- Ephesians 2:8–9
- Titus 3:3–8

Key verse: 'Grace and peace to you from God our Father and the Lord Jesus Christ, who gave himself for our sins to rescue us from the present evil age, according to the will of our God and Father …' Galatians 1:3–4

Focus: There is only one gospel.

Opening Our Eyes

Discredit the messenger and you discredit the message.
The Galatian Christians had received Paul as if he were
an angel from heaven, and when he proclaimed to them
the good news of God's grace in Christ they believed him.
The life-changing Holy Spirit fell on these new converts
and they experienced many amazing miracles. What had
happened to them was a genuine work of God and it was
bearing good fruit.

That is, until other preachers turned up; Judaeans
purporting to be from the apostle James.

It's all very well receiving Christ's forgiveness, these
people said, but you can't be a full believer, a true
member of the chosen race, unless you embrace the
Jewish religious law as well – including the calendar of
festivals and the rite of circumcision. Paul should have
told you this. Why didn't he? Maybe it's because he
was not one of the Twelve. Perhaps he got his message
second-hand from Antioch. Or does he want to keep you
as second-class saints because you are not Jewish pure
bloods like him?

Paul is astounded at the Galatian believers' naivety in
giving credence to this nonsense, and so soon after their
conversion. For a start, he is a true apostle. His own
remarkable conversion is well attested. It also included a
direct revelation of the risen Christ, the One who chose
and commissioned him to proclaim the gospel and to
suffer for it. Likewise, his message of salvation through
faith in Christ alone came straight from God, without any
human intervention. This is the authentic gospel believed
by Christians everywhere, whatever their background. It is
not just Paul's own idea or that of a few cranks.

These Judaisers, or Jew-makers, on the other hand, are false messengers who represent a terrible danger to your faith. Their message so perverts the true gospel that it turns into 'another gospel', a 'dyspel', bad news, not good news. Allow their teaching to infect you and it will destroy your pure faith. Instead of being rescued from this passing world and its evils, you will have jumped right back in and lost everything you have gained.

The issues are so serious that there can be no compromise or half measures. These false teachers are a menace. Anathematise them! Have nothing more to do with either them or their destructive deceits. Leave them to the judgment of God. Never mind their supposed credentials – as if they really represented the apostle James! Even if they claim to be angels from heaven – even if it were I myself teaching you – distance yourself from anyone who teaches a message other than justification by faith in Christ alone.

Truth matters. Treat the patient with the wrong medicine and the patient dies. This is not simply Paul's opinion, and it has nothing to do with his own reputation. He is a servant of Christ, no more, no less. He has no authority to teach other than what Christ taught him, and that goes for everyone else with him. Christ died and rose again to free us from our sins, so that we could become a new creation – children of Adam miraculously made children of God. Jesus has freed us from the vices and evils of this transitory world so that we might inherit an eternal kingdom. Don't allow this message of pure grace to be adulterated with law-works of your own, otherwise Christ's sacrificial death on the cross is reduced to nothing.

Discussion Starters

1. From this passage, what does Paul consider to be the heart of the Christian gospel?

   _____

   _____

   _____

   _____

   _____

2. What do you think constitutes the evils of our contemporary society?

   _____

   _____

   _____

   _____

   _____

3. How do we know if a preacher or teacher is genuine?

   _____

   _____

   _____

   _____

   _____

4. Where do you see the 'gospel' of law manifested in the Church, in politics and in society?

   _____

   _____

   _____

   _____

   _____

5. How do we contend for the truth without being merely contentious?

_____

_____

_____

_____

_____

6. Explain why Paul is so passionate about the integrity and exclusivity of the gospel message.

_____

_____

_____

_____

_____

7. What does it mean for us as Christian witnesses to be in the world, but not of the world?

_____

_____

_____

_____

_____

Personal Application

Do we share Paul's passion for truth and authenticity? Does truth even matter in a pluralistic society where anything goes and your truth is your truth, and my truth is my truth? Is there such a thing as 'true truth' any more? Don't all religious rivers flow into the same sea?

Every generation of Christians has had to believe their beliefs – 'to contend for the faith that was once for all entrusted to the saints' (Jude 3). Today is no exception. This gospel of grace alone is 'the power of God for the salvation of everyone who believes' (Rom. 1:16). It is exclusive truth, but gloriously inclusive truth for all who will receive it.

Seeing Jesus in the Scriptures

Jesus is the heart of the gospel; it is not a doctrine, nor a creed, nor a code of conduct, but a Person who died for our sins and whom God the Father raised from the dead. He is 'the Son of God, who loved me and gave himself for me' (Gal. 2:20). We can add nothing to His work of redemption. What we can do is receive it in grateful faith.

Jesus did this so that we should be delivered from not just the corruption of our society, but from our identity with it. We are dead to the world, and the world is dead to us. That doesn't mean withdrawing from the world; on the contrary, we are in it to win it, but we are no longer of it. Instead, we are members of the new creation in Christ Jesus.

WEEK 2

Authority and Authenticity

Opening Icebreaker

Act this out. One of you is Peter; another is Paul. Two others are Pharisees, out of the room. The rest are 50% Jewish Christians and 50% Gentile Christians. You are happily eating biscuits together with Peter and Paul. When the two Pharisees enter the room, Peter and all the Jewish believers separate themselves from the Gentile believers and eat elsewhere. How do you feel about this?

Bible Readings

- Galatians 1:11–2:21
- Acts 15:1–11
- Philippians 3:2–9
- Acts 9:1–31
- Romans 6:1–11

Key verse: 'For through the law I died to the law so that I might live for God. I have been crucified with Christ and I no longer live, but Christ lives in me. The life I live in the body, I live by faith in the Son of God, who loved me and gave himself for me.' Galatians 2:19–20

Focus: Authentic living ministers authentic faith.

Opening Our Eyes

There was no greater expert than Paul when it came to living by law, and no one less likely to embrace the gospel of grace. A rigid Pharisee, a fanatical persecutor of the Church, he was carving out a path to high office within the Jewish elite. Then Jesus, risen from the dead, met him and called him to do the unthinkable; to preach Christ among the Gentiles. It's not something Paul would have invented for himself, nor copied from others!

Paul preached Christ in Damascus for three years subsequent to his conversion, but he had no contact with Jerusalem. Then he visited Peter for fifteen days, and also met James. Fourteen years later he and his companions, Barnabas and Titus, returned to Jerusalem. False brothers had infiltrated the apostolic band to discredit its work. Rumours abounded. Something had to be done. Paul called for a private meeting with the church leaders in Jerusalem to explain what they were preaching. No way was he preaching Christ plus law. Even Greek Titus did not have to be circumcised in Jerusalem! The Jerusalem leaders added no extras to Paul's message because they were in agreement with it. They recognised Paul's calling to preach the same gospel to the Gentiles as Peter did to the Jews. James, Peter and John blessed their mission, asking only that they cared for the poor.

All seemed fine until Peter visited the church in Antioch. Initially, he ate happily with his non-Jewish brethren. Then the Jew-makers arrived and Peter compromised by refusing to eat any longer with Gentiles. Others followed his example, prompting Paul to mount a public challenge. Why would Peter, a Jewish Christian who normally lived like a Gentile, suddenly insist that Gentiles should now live like Jews to be included at the meal table? For that was surely the implication of his actions.

Paul's appeal is passionate and intensely personal. We all agree that Gentile sinners can be saved only by faith in Christ – just as we Jews are. Neither party can be saved by law-works. Gentile sinners already know this: they had neither the law nor chosen race status to begin with. It was justification by faith, or nothing. We ethnic Jews, raised believing that obeying the law justified us before God, discovered that it doesn't work because our hearts were corrupt, just like those of Gentile sinners. We abandoned the futile law-works route and put our faith in Christ instead.

Does admitting our failure redefine us Jews as Gentile sinners, thereby making Christ a 'sinner status' promoter? No way! But be warned, if we put law-works back into our lives, which we already know we can't keep, then we re-categorise *ourselves* as lawbreaking Jews. That's as bad as Gentile sinner status!

What then of the law? I have died to it, says Paul; it no longer governs my existence. My old life of self-righteousness, condemnation and failure is over. I am dead, crucified with Christ! What then of my mortal life? Hallelujah, Christ is risen! He now lives in me, and I in Him! This is my new identity. I am not a Gentile sinner; I am not a Jewish legalist. I am a 'Christian'. Christ the faithful One living in me defines who I am and how I live. Living any other way will nullify the grace of God; for if I re-establish law as the basis for righteousness then Christ's death is worthless.

Discussion Starters

1. Why do you think the apostle Paul is so often misunderstood and reviled?

_____

_____

_____

_____

_____

2. Paul and his apostolic band, and Peter and the Jerusalem apostles, agreed on one gospel for all. What are the key elements of that gospel?

_____

_____

_____

_____

_____

3. How would you explain the term 'justification by faith' to a non-Christian friend?

_____

_____

_____

_____

_____

4. Why can't righteousness before God be attained by means of keeping the law?

_____

_____

_____

_____

_____

5. What characterised the Judaisers, or Jew-makers, and why were they wrong?

_____

_____

_____

_____

_____

6. What was Peter's compromise and why was Paul's rebuke so important for the future of the gospel?

_____

_____

_____

_____

_____

7. What does it mean to be crucified with Christ and to be raised with Him?

_____

_____

_____

_____

_____

Personal Application

Peter's inconsistency unwittingly put the entire gospel at risk. By compromising fellowship with Gentile believers he played into the hands of the enemies of true faith. Our behaviour speaks more loudly than our words. It is not enough to believe our beliefs; we have to live our beliefs.

Specifically, there can be no class, gender, racial or cultural segregation between fellow Christians, no refusing to mix in equal fellowship with those of a different denomination or stream to our own. Nor may we seek to impose our cultural rules on others. If we are saved by grace alone then we must live by grace alone and offer that grace freely to all who fall within our sphere of influence. Authentic living ministers authentic faith.

Seeing Jesus in the Scriptures

The law put Jesus to death on our behalf. Since you can't hurt a dead man or enslave him any further, Christ is totally free from the law. By identifying with Him in His death, we are set free from the law as surely as He is. His faith in the Father raised Him from the dead, and by identifying with Him in His resurrection we share His eternal life. Christ now lives in us and seeks to live His redemptive life through us.

Letting Christ live in us, directing our ways, shaping our character, and inspiring our lives, is a free and willing response to the Son of God who loved us, and who gave Himself for us. Nothing could be further removed from the rigid, uptight and downright miserable life of the rule driven.

WEEK 3

The Law and the Promise

Opening Icebreaker

Share recent experiences of the Holy Spirit at work in your lives. What might you have done to earn these blessings?

Bible Readings

- Galatians 3:1–18
- John 8:56–58
- Genesis 12:1–3
- Romans 4:1–3, 9–17

Key verse: 'So those who have faith are blessed along with Abraham, the man of faith. All who rely on observing the law are under a curse …' Galatians 3:9–10

Focus: The law puts us under a curse; faith in the promise blesses us with the Holy Spirit.

Opening Our Eyes

Paul has affirmed that there is only one gospel for Jews and Gentiles alike – a gospel of justification by faith in Christ apart from works. All true apostles are agreed on this. So, what is happening to you Galatian believers, Paul asks? Someone has bewitched you, mesmerised you with lies. You have heard and believed the authentic gospel of Christ crucified to make us right with God. The Holy Spirit has fallen on you, confirming that you are truly children of God through faith in Christ. You are genuine charismatic believers who have suffered for your faith, and yet are experiencing God's miraculous works in your midst. Was any of this the result of your law-works? Of course not! So, how foolish to imagine that having started by faith you could now complete your journey by works.

Take a look at Abraham. His story is recorded in the Law of Moses – the law these Jew-makers are so keen on. Abraham is the father of faith because he believed God, and it was credited to him as righteousness. Surely the true children of Abraham are those who share Abraham's faith, irrespective of their ethnic background. These are the ones blessed by the Spirit of promise. Indeed, these scriptures, penned by Moses the lawgiver no less, record that God proclaimed the gospel to Abraham, promising in advance that people of all nations would be justified by faith.

By contrast, all those who try to justify themselves by their law-works live under a curse. The reason is simple: you have to live an absolutely perfect life, on the outside, and on the inside. No one can, and no one does.

Secondly, because the law by definition is not based on faith and yet righteousness can only come about by faith, to resort to law-works is to miss the way completely. It's a bit like boasting a qualification in geography when the job application clearly requires a qualification in maths. You don't even get an interview!

All very well, but can merely believing make us right with God? The law is made of sterner stuff. It demands personal accountability, it finds us guilty and it sets a price to be paid for sin. It also excludes the lawless Gentiles. Precisely so, Paul agrees. We are cursed, indeed!

But there is a Redeemer. Christ, the innocent One, took the law's curse on Himself. He submitted Himself to judgment for our sins and took our punishment. They hung Him on a tree as an outcast criminal. The price is paid; the curse is broken, and we are free to receive the blessing of Abraham. Thanks to Christ's redemptive work, all Gentiles can become children of Abraham. God's promise to bless all nations through Him is fulfilled when we, Jews and Gentiles, place our faith in Christ. From that moment on, we become family, and legitimate heirs to the blessing of the promised Holy Spirit.

How sure are we that this is true? Take the example of human covenants. We know that such covenants are binding upon the various human parties concerned. Well, this is God's covenant promise, and it was made to Abraham and to his seed. There is only one Seed and that is Christ. The law came 430 years later but it cannot override the precedent of this original faith covenant. A promise is a promise, and those that God makes are unbreakable, of that we may be certain!

Discussion Starters

1. Where do you think we might find in our modern world the same subtle bewitchment that led the Galatians astray?

_____

_____

_____

_____

_____

2. What steps do we need to take in order to receive the fullness of the Holy Spirit?

_____

_____

_____

_____

_____

3. What do you think God intended when He gave a promise to Abraham in Genesis 12:1–3?

_____

_____

_____

_____

_____

4. Why are all those who try to justify themselves by law-works under a curse?

_____

_____

_____

_____

_____

5. Why was it necessary for Jesus to become cursed when He died on the cross?

_____

_____

_____

_____

_____

6. Why do you think we like to offset our bad deeds with our good deeds?

_____

_____

_____

_____

_____

7. If Jesus is the promised Seed of the woman what does that make us, and why?

_____

_____

_____

_____

_____

Personal Application

Deception deceives; and nothing deceives more than law-based salvation. The temptation to improve our standing before God, to raise our sense of self-worth, to create badges of belonging by our own efforts, is rife. But it is a path of damnation; either we will grow proud and self-righteous because we think we are succeeding, or we will fall into guilt, condemnation and despair because we think we have failed. If we choose this way of life we will be living on a wretched seesaw of blessing and cursing, of obedience and failure.

Praise God, Jesus came to smash the seesaw in pieces! In its place, we have received the Holy Spirit of promise who guarantees our sonship and empowers us to live transcendent lives of gratitude and love. It really is as simple as that, if only we realised it!

Seeing Jesus in the Scriptures

Jesus is the promised Seed of the woman first prophesied in Genesis 3:15. The Old Testament is really the earthly story of the heavenly Jerusalem's pregnancy, and of the struggle to bring the Seed to birth in the face of satanic opposition (see Rev. 12:1–5). Yet God's purpose cannot be thwarted and in due time He sent His Son, as He promised, to be our Redeemer. The Seed was wounded, but in the process He destroyed Satan's power, liberating us from our bondage to the law of sin and death. The spirit of servile fear is replaced by the Spirit of promise when we receive by faith the work of Jesus on our behalf.

WEEK 4

The Slaves and the Sons

Opening Icebreaker

Each member of the group is given a written charter:
'I hereby declare that [name] is released from spiritual
slavery and is granted the freeborn status of a son of God
through faith in Jesus Christ. Signed Abba Father.' What
does this mean for each one in the group?

Bible Readings

- Galatians 3:19–4:7
- Romans 3:19–20
- Hebrews 2:10–16
- John 1:12–13
- Ephesians 1:13–14

Key verse: 'You are all sons of God through faith in Christ
Jesus, for all of you who were baptised into Christ have
clothed yourselves with Christ. There is neither Jew nor
Greek, slave nor free, male nor female, for you are all
one in Christ Jesus. If you belong to Christ, then you are
Abraham's seed, and heirs according to the promise.'
Galatians 3:26–29

Focus: Faith in Christ changes our status from slavery to
sonship.

Opening Our Eyes

It is hard to overestimate the importance of the law to the Jews. Like the American Constitution or the Bible or the Koran it formed the foundation for morality, religion, life, identity and society. To challenge the law was to challenge the very basis for existence. It was tantamount to blasphemy.

Paul must answer this charge. If God had always intended that salvation should be by grace through faith, then why did He bother instituting the law with its commandments and ordinances in the first place? Is the law in mortal conflict with the promise? Can you simply dismiss something that was given by God – through angels – and delivered by no less a person than Moses?

Absolutely not! The law is good and conceivably there could have been a law that imparted eternal life. There wasn't such a law because that was never the purpose of the law. God gave the law to fulfil a necessary but intermediate role in human affairs. The law defines the sinfulness of the human heart; it tells us when we are right and it tells us when we are wrong. We know where we stand before God and man, because we have a written standard.

The sad but honest reality is that we are all prisoners of sin, and the law is the jailer, keeping us in check. It has been like that for centuries and so it might have continued but for one astounding fact. The promised Seed has come! A new age has dawned. It is time for the prisoners to walk free, and they may do so by putting their faith in Jesus Christ. The law has done its job. It has convicted us of sin and shown us the futility of trying to save ourselves by our own efforts. It has led us to Christ to be justified by faith.

For that reason, we no longer need the law's supervision. We have ceased to be slaves. We have become sons of God through our faith in Christ. This is our new status. Baptised into Christ, we are clothed with Christ; we are defined by who He is. The old legal divisions between Jews and Gentiles, slaves and free, male and female are rendered redundant. We are reconstituted as one new man in Christ – Abraham's seed and legitimate heirs to the promise.

This was always to be our destiny, but our time under the law was like childhood. The child may have legal rights to the entire estate, yet he will not be allowed to exercise those rights until he comes of age. Meanwhile, our tutors and guardians have the job of preparing us for adulthood. We are forced to go to school and learn the alphabet, the rules and regulations, the basic sums. The law was a necessary slavery!

However, all that has changed. In fulfilment of the divine plan, God has broken into history in Jesus of Nazareth. His Son (fully divine), the Seed of the woman (fully human), born in the Jewish jailhouse, has paid the redemption price so that we might enter the adult privileges of sonship.

This is why we have received the Holy Spirit. Just as the Spirit witnessed at Jesus' baptism that He was the Son of God, so it is with us. The fact that the Spirit of Christ cries 'Abba, Father' within us is a sign that we are no longer slaves to sin but are sons and heirs with Him.

Discussion Starters

1. What do you understand to be the true and the false purposes of the Law of Moses?

_____

_____

_____

_____

_____

2. Why don't we need the law's supervision once we have put our faith in Christ?

_____

_____

_____

_____

_____

3. What happened when you were baptised into Christ?

_____

_____

_____

_____

_____

4. How would you explain to a Jewish friend that Jesus is the promised Seed?

_____

_____

_____

_____

_____

5. How would you explain to someone involved in a ritualistic religion, like Freemasonry or Wicca, the freedom to grow up that faith in Christ offers?

_____

_____

_____

_____

_____

6. What is your experience of the sealing of the Holy Spirit and its impact on your sense of sonship?

_____

_____

_____

_____

_____

7. What does being all one in Christ Jesus mean in practice for your church and its relationship with other churches?

_____

_____

_____

_____

_____

Personal Application

Christianity is a world faith, embracing as it does people of every culture, ethnicity and social standing. It is our glory that none are excluded or given a lower status than others; we are all one in Christ Jesus.

How vital it is, then, that we treat one another in such a manner. The world scorns our divisions; people will not forgive us if they sense any arrogance on our part that makes them feel second-class, unwanted, unloved. Sadly, our society is filled with people who once attended church but who now feel rejected because they sensed we didn't really want them.

Let us ensure that there is no cliquishness in our churches, no despising of those who don't quite fit our preferences, no hurtful words that might cause the young to stumble.

Seeing Jesus in the Scriptures

God's timing is always perfect. He is the Lord of history, the ruler of the nations who enthrones and dethrones according to His eternal purposes in Christ. Jesus came at the perfect time and in the perfect place, just as it had been prophesied. Roman government ensured good communications, the Greeks provided a common language, Israel supplied the context for His ministry of redemption – and Mary was the ideal mum to give Jesus His human nature. Or, to put it another way, Jesus was conceived out of wedlock to a young teenager, in occupied territory, under a brutal totalitarian dictatorship, surrounded by immoral pagan idolaters, in a culture characterised by the most rigid religious tyranny.

Like we say, God's timing is always perfect. It still is!

WEEK 5

The Slave Woman and the Free Woman

Opening Icebreaker

What 'gods' and other things did we serve before we knew the Lord? In what ways did these false things hold us in bondage?

Bible Readings

- Galatians 4:8–31
- 1 Timothy 4:1–5
- Revelation 12:1–6, 13–17

- Genesis 21:8–13
- Hebrews 12:1–3, 22–24

Key verse: "'Get rid of the slave woman and her son, for the slave woman's son will never share in the inheritance with the free woman's son.' Therefore, brothers, we are not children of the slave woman, but of the free woman.' Galatians 4:30–31

Focus: Law and grace are incompatible.

Opening Our Eyes

Primitive religion does not mean better religion, any more than the experience of a child is better than that of an adult. Everyone knows that it is impossible to keep the law perfectly, but in a desperate effort to compensate for our human imperfections, we create even more rules and regulations, as if this will somehow help! Driven by despair we embrace superstition. Already in bondage to the law, we sell ourselves to pathetic demons, hoping that keeping our little rules and rituals will bring us luck and keep divine retribution at bay. Lucky charms, touching wood, invoking oaths, dietary regulations, auspicious days – anything to stave off our fears and our failings.

Paul is deeply grieved at this apparent waste of his labours, and he makes an impassioned appeal to his readers. Why would anyone want to exchange an intimate personal relationship with God for this primitive religious rubbish? In spite of his physical infirmity (possibly some form of eye problem), the Galatians had received him as one of God's messengers. He had been to them a loved and honoured mouthpiece and a representative of Christ. They had embraced the truth of the gospel wholeheartedly. Such was their love and respect for Paul that they would have given their own eyes to relieve him of his ailment.

How come they were now prepared to treat him as an enemy when all he had done was tell them the truth? These Jew-makers with their message of the so-called higher way were zealous but they did not have any real care for God's people. Indeed, they were actually excluding them from the gospel and from the rest of Christ's Church. Unlike them, Paul loves these people the way a mother loves her own babies. Must he now go through labour pains again to form Christ in them? How he yearns to be present with them to resolve his doubts about their condition!

Turning his attention to the Jew-makers, Paul challenges the implications of their teaching. He refers them back to the life of Abraham, their spiritual and natural ancestor. Abraham had two sons, one by the slave woman, Hagar, and the other by his wife, Sarah. The first conception was natural and was Abraham's own faithless effort at producing an heir. The conception of Isaac was nothing less than miraculous, given the age of the parents. The birth of Isaac was the fulfilment of God's promise to provide Abraham with a legitimate heir.

Using this analogy, Paul applies this well-known story to two covenants. Hagar's son, Ishmael, represents Mount Sinai where the law was given, and Jerusalem where the law has its headquarters. This is the prison house of spiritual bondage.

Sarah, meanwhile, represents the joyous and fecund heavenly Jerusalem who is the eternal free mother of all those who put their faith in Christ. These believers – former Jews and Gentiles – are the true spiritual line of Abraham; they are all children of promise.

There can be no compatibility between the children of the flesh and the children of the promise. It may have seemed harsh that Abraham cast out Hagar and Ishmael, but he was trying to put right a bad mistake. In the same way, the Galatians will need decisively to reject the teaching of these Jew-makers. If they don't, these beloved brethren will fall back into religious bondage and throw away their entire spiritual inheritance in Christ. The choice is as stark as that.

Discussion Starters

1. How would you explain to a superstitious person that they are in slavery to the basic principles (or elemental spirits) of this world? What hope can you offer them?

_____

_____

_____

_____

_____

2. Name some of the superstitious and legalistic regulations that people adopt in our current society.

_____

_____

_____

_____

_____

3. How would you defend and explain your personal relationship with God when you are such an insignificant speck in a vast universe?

_____

_____

_____

_____

_____

4. How may we celebrate special days without falling into the trap of the Jew-makers?

_____

_____

_____

_____

_____

5. How would you explain Paul's analogy of the two covenants to an Arab friend, and to a Jewish friend?

_____

_____

_____

_____

_____

6. What are the similarities and the contrasts between the earthly Jerusalem and the heavenly Jerusalem?

_____

_____

_____

_____

_____

7. Why do religious and secular legalists oppose grace and truth so forcefully?

_____

_____

_____

_____

_____

Personal Application

We should never underestimate the subtlety of the devil. Revelation 12 graphically illustrates his hatred and persecution of the heavenly mother Jerusalem and the Seed. Having not been able to destroy either mother or child, he continues to make war on the rest of her offspring, that is, on us.

Satan is most effective when he can seduce us back into superstitious bondage under the guise of spiritual self-improvement. It is easy to criticise believers who are bound to set forms of worship while forgetting the petty personal rules that we make for ourselves. These might range from wearing lucky charms to compulsive religious habits, to denying ourselves certain foods, and sexual asceticism. These things can become substitutes for a living relationship with God our Father. We need to examine our lives and separate ourselves from such superstitious, legalistic bondage.

Seeing Jesus in the Scriptures

Jesus is the descendant of Isaac; He is the Son of promise birthed from the heavenly Jerusalem through the instrumentality of Mary. Just as Ishmael persecuted Isaac, so the earthly Jerusalem persecuted Jesus. The law will always oppose grace and truth, because grace and truth render the law redundant and humble our self-righteous instincts.

In spite of persecution, the Son of promise lives for ever! Jesus has returned to His heavenly mother, Jerusalem above, where He now dwells with all His glorified saints. This is the great cloud of witnesses whom one day we shall join (see Heb. 12:1–3, 22–24). His destiny is our destiny, His hope is our hope, His city will be our city.

WEEK 6

Liberty and Love

Opening Icebreaker

Give some testimonies about how you have been shown love by the Christian community.

Bible Readings

- Galatians 5:1–15
- Luke 10:25–37
- Romans 13:8–10
- Mark 12:28–34
- John 15:9–17

Key verse: 'You, my brothers, were called to be free. But do not use your freedom to indulge the sinful nature; rather, serve one another in love.' Galatians 5:13

Focus: Christian liberty is not licence. It is the freedom to love.

Opening Our Eyes

The decision to observe Jewish fasts and rituals was reversible. Circumcision was not. Those who underwent the rite would become de facto Jewish proselytes and their actions would alienate them from Christ. Having freed themselves from slavery to the law they would walk right back into the prison from which faith in Christ had delivered them. They would be obliged, like the Israelites in Egypt, to make bricks without straw for a building that would never benefit them. Christ would become irrelevant. Those who have taken this path have fallen from grace.

Let there be no doubt about this. Paul, a circumcised Jewish believer himself, makes it crystal clear. The choice is simple: either be circumcised and take on the yoke of perfect obedience to the law, which will alienate you from Christ and all the benefits of His grace, or stand firm in faith, inspired by the Spirit to live secure in your divine acceptance through the righteousness of Christ. In truth, physical circumcision or otherwise is no longer relevant. All that matters is faith expressing itself through love.

Paul's passion is evident throughout this epistle. His children in the faith were doing so well in the race of life. Somebody has cut in on them, breaking their stride and forcing them off track. Such a person doesn't represent Christ or the truth. It certainly isn't Paul! Anyone suggesting otherwise is speaking nonsense. If Paul was preaching circumcision why was he being persecuted? Surely it was because he was determined to preach nothing but Christ and Him crucified as the only hope of salvation.

The Galatians must act; this poisonous yeast is capable of infecting the entire work of God. Paul is sure that they will see sense. As for the person causing this confusion, well, let him be judged accordingly. Do these agitators really think that mutilating their bodies can make them right with God? If so, why don't they go the whole way and castrate themselves entirely!

Having dismissed the Jew-makers and their perverse arguments, Paul now addresses the underlying issue. If we abandon the law as a basis for life, surely that will lead us down the path of licentiousness. In other words, those of Jewish background will become sinners and those of Gentile background will remain sinners. We will be no different from the corrupt pagan world around us. Worse still, our so-called righteousness through faith will be a hollow hypocrisy. Surely belief needs a framework of rules to keep us on track. The law must set the standard for our faith.

Not so, says Paul. God's people are called to freedom from the law and its demands but this is not an invitation to lawlessness or licence. Instead, it is a call to serve one another with sacrificial love. The law was never intended to be an end in itself, nor a means of self-justification. Love is the whole meaning of the law and love is more powerful than the law. Love your neighbour as yourself and you fulfil the law while being free from the law. This is absolutely in accord with Christ's teaching.

These Jew-makers, on the other hand, are having the opposite effect. Their call to self salvation, with its inherent selfishness and competitiveness, its elitism and pride, and its ceaseless arguments and divisions, is turning people into spiritual cannibals! Watch out, Paul warns, or there will be nothing left of you but stripped bones.

Discussion Starters

1. Why do you think taking the route of law-works alienates us from Christ?

_____

_____

_____

_____

_____

2. Why do you say that faith in Christ is sufficient for acceptance with God and the transformation of your life?

_____

_____

_____

_____

_____

3. How do you address the statement, 'It's not what you do but what you believe that matters'? What is true about it, and what is false?

_____

_____

_____

_____

_____

4. What do you say to the person who argues that they do their best to live a good life?

_____

_____

_____

_____

_____

5. How might we find ourselves devouring one another? What can we do to avoid this?

_____
_____
_____
_____
_____

6. What does it mean in practice to live by faith expressing itself through love?

_____
_____
_____
_____
_____

7. Discuss ways that we can be better Good Samaritans in our daily lives.

_____
_____
_____
_____
_____

Personal Application

Middle-class 'decency' and 'standards' can so easily become a supposed basis for acceptance with God. This was the problem with the Pharisees in Jesus' day. With less than subtle irony Jesus told them that He had 'not come to call the righteous, but sinners to repentance' (Luke 5:32). We must beware lest cultural and class advantages fool us into thinking that we are better than we are. Our hope and trust for salvation must be in Christ alone, whatever our background.

We must also ensure that those without social advantages do not feel inferior or disadvantaged within church culture. Better the person who has to draw heavily on the grace of God to get anywhere than the person who has no need for grace and gets nowhere.

Seeing Jesus in the Scriptures

Jesus 'went around doing good and healing all who were under the power of the devil' (Acts 10:38). His life exemplified doing and teaching (Acts 1:1), and He calls us to do the same. His parables of the Good Samaritan and the Sheep and the Goats, His feeding of the 5,000 and the 4,000, reveal faith expressed in practical love as the true manifestation of the kingdom. People believed His message because they saw His works demonstrating His words.

The liberal gospel of yesteryear appeared to replace saving faith with good works and led many evangelicals to abandon this so-called 'social gospel' in favour of gospel preaching. Thankfully, biblical churches today are engaging with their local communities, recognising relationship building as the Christlike foundation for sharing the gospel.

WEEK 7

The Spirit and the Flesh

Opening Icebreaker

Each person chooses one of the fruit of the Spirit that they would especially like to see more of in their own life. Pray briefly for each one to see that fulfilled.

Bible Readings

- Galatians 5:16–6:18
- Matthew 7:15–20
- Ezekiel 36:24–27
- Romans 13:3–5, 8–10

Key verse: 'The one who sows to please his sinful nature, from that nature will reap destruction; the one who sows to please the Spirit, from the Spirit will reap eternal life.' Galatians 6:8

Focus: The way of the sinful nature produces death; the way of the Spirit produces life.

Opening Our Eyes

The gospel of grace isn't just a matter of personal piety; it has social and political implications. A society based on the acts of the sinful nature will soon self-destruct, or find it necessary to impose Draconian laws on its citizens. Finding a balance between personal freedom and the need to restrain the excesses of self-interest is the fundamental tension for all legislators. Ironically, although laws may deal with the outward manifestations of the sinful nature, they cannot cure the heart. A society cannot be made good by law.

There is only one cure, only one way to a truly good society, and that is the way of the Spirit. The law simply does not have the power to produce goodness; the best it can do is to restrain evil. However, the Holy Spirit transforms the human heart and makes possible a virtuous life. When we acknowledge our inability to save ourselves and, instead, put our faith in Christ, the gift of the Holy Spirit sets us free to love. We are no longer bound by law, and we are no longer bound by sin.

If we choose to live by the Spirit we will not gratify the desires of the sinful nature because there is no compatibility between the two. As we allow the Holy Spirit to lead us, He will cultivate within our hearts the fruit of a virtuous life that far transcends the impotence of the law. Living this way is consistent with our identification with Christ. We crucified the sinful nature and its cravings when we put our faith in Jesus. If that's how we started then that's how to continue, walking in step with the Holy Spirit.

What does this unique way of life in the Spirit mean in practice?

It frees us from arrogance and conceit. We will no longer be vying with one another for position, nor will we be judging one another. If somebody commits a public sin, the spiritually mature will seek to restore the fallen brother or sister in a spirit of humility. We will recognise our own vulnerabilities as we share the burdens of others, at the same time taking responsibility for our own actions and maintaining a humble heart.

It is the path of wisdom and truth. God's fundamental laws of the universe cannot be flouted; we reap what we sow. Sow to the sinful nature by legalism or lawlessness and we reap the seeds of our own destruction. Sow in accord with the Holy Spirit and we reap eternal life. There are no other options. Our loving practical service for the benefit of believers and unbelievers alike will produce a good harvest. Just stick with it! Better to be weary doing good to others than to wear ourselves out trying to attain our own righteousness, or slaving away at sin.

The Jew-makers were cowards, trying to avoid the offence of the cross. Instead, they wanted to boast about the number of proselytes they had made. Paul will only glory in the cross of Christ that delivered him from the ways of the world. Circumcision and uncircumcision are no longer relevant. A new creation is emerging; anyone who is in Christ is part of that new creation. Blessings upon this, the true Israel of God. End of argument. Paul has been there, done it, proved it, and has the scars to show for it. He wishes only the grace of Christ to bless his brethren.

Discussion Starters

1. What does the Holy Spirit do that the law cannot do?

_____
_____
_____
_____

2. In the light of Romans 13:3–5, 8–10, what would you like to say to your politicians about the laws they make and how they apply them?

_____
_____
_____
_____
_____

3. How would you explain to a non-Christian friend the difference the Holy Spirit makes to your life?

_____
_____
_____
_____
_____

4. What do you think constitutes a virtuous or truly good life in practice?

_____
_____
_____
_____
_____

5. What does it mean to sow to please the sinful nature, and what does it mean to sow to please the Spirit?

_____

_____

_____

_____

_____

6. What should be our attitude towards a brother or sister caught in sin?

_____

_____

_____

_____

_____

7. Explain why the cross of Christ has rendered religion redundant and replaced it with a new creation?

_____

_____

_____

_____

Personal Application

Our Christian lives should be virtuous; that is, we should manifest the fruit of the Spirit in all our relationships. We do so simply by walking in the Spirit day by day. This is our free choice as those who have crucified the sinful nature with Christ.

The choice is to determine that we plant only good seed. This means refusing to indulge the sinful nature; it also means refusing to strive at making ourselves holy. Yielding to the Holy Spirit is a learned art, but doing so will produce a good harvest as we serve those around us in love.

We won't always get it right, but we can help one another. Sometimes our fellow believers will sin badly. In those cases we should do our best to bring them to repentance and restoration, but do so with an attitude of heart that recognises our own frailties. We are, after all, responsible for our own actions.

Seeing Jesus in the Scriptures

The bottom line of Paul's argument is this: either we choose to boast in the cross of Christ or we choose to boast in our own self-righteousness. The Jew-makers wanted to show how clever they were; we want to glory in how great Jesus is. 'Forbid it, Lord, that I should boast save in the death of Christ my God.'

The death and resurrection of Christ spells the end of our spiritual bondage to the world of lawlessness and legalism. Jesus is the firstborn of the new creation; He is the new Israel of God, and by grace, so are we.

Leader's Notes

Week 1: Good News and Bad News

Paul's letter to the Galatians is one of the most important books ever written. It addresses the question: What must I do to be saved? The answer is what makes the Christian faith totally distinct from all other belief systems. Start this series by reading the Introduction to your group, so that they have an overview of this great book and its central theme of freedom in Christ through faith alone.

Opening Icebreaker

The Opening Icebreaker presents a far-fetched scenario, but the point it demonstrates is a serious one, that wrong treatment is not a matter of opinion but of life and death. It's the same with the gospel; not just any fine sounding message will do; people's eternal life is at stake.

Aim of the Session

Make sure you understand the background and the issues. The Jew-makers were a constant thorn in the side of the apostle Paul and they used every possible means to discredit him. These supposed Christian Jews vehemently opposed the message of salvation by faith alone. Dogging Paul's steps, they stirred up violent reaction against him whenever they could. Plausible, deceitful manipulators, they paid lip service to Christ, thereby gaining an entrance into the churches, but their real intention was to seduce people away from Christ and back into Judaism.

Paul is not worried so much for his own reputation as for the wellbeing of the young Christians in Galatia. These

Judaisers, or Jew-makers, wanted to add Jewish law to the gospel, not just the religious calendar and food laws but also the rite of circumcision. In effect, this would render the work of Christ null and void and result in Jewish Christians reverting to Judaism and the Gentile Christians becoming Jewish proselytes. It would mark an early end to the uniqueness of the Christian message and ensure its demise. This is why Paul is so passionate about the need to deal with these false teachers and their teaching. There can be no compromise on life and death matters.

After doing the readings, read the Opening Our Eyes section.

Discussion Starter 1 is best answered from verses 3–5. The evils of our contemporary society referred to in Discussion Starter 2 include not only the obvious sins but also legalistic religions, superstitions and the legal repression of civil liberties.

The Church has repeatedly been infiltrated and infected by those who wish to add to the gospel, either consciously or unconsciously. Use Discussion Starters 3 and 4 to explore these dangers. Ensure that your group understands that their faith must rest exclusively and completely in Christ alone. Adding Jewish cultural practices or rituals to enhance our Christian faith is as wrong as adding pagan techniques for spiritual self-improvement.

Discussion Starters 5, 6 and 7 address our stance as Christians in contemporary society. We inhabit a world that boasts of tolerance but is often intolerant of Christian truth claims. Sadly, in reaction to this, some Christians are frankly obnoxious in their witness. Use these Discussion Starters to explore how we can stand firm for the truth yet live qualitatively different lives in the world, so that we are winsome rather than loathsome. Encourage your group to use examples from their own experience.

Read the Personal Application and Seeing Jesus sections at this point and end your session focusing on Jesus as the heart of the gospel. Pray together to thank Him for what He has done for us, and ask Him to help us to bear a good testimony to Him by our lives, our words and our deeds.

Week 2: Authority and Authenticity

Opening Icebreaker

In performing this simple Icebreaker your aim is to demonstrate the inconsistency of Christian segregation and its effect on those who are suddenly made to feel second-class by the behaviour of the superior class.

Aim of the Session

In all these sessions get into the habit of sharing out the Bible readings with others in your group. Read out the key verse and the focus.

The apostle Paul's conversion was nothing short of miraculous. As a leading persecutor of the Church he was the least likely person to become the greatest exponent of the gospel. This alone was sufficient to outrage his opponents; their champion had changed sides. The attacks were personal, charging Paul with being a false messenger, someone who got his message second-hand and who was not one of the original twelve apostles. They accused him of inconsistency, saying that he preached Christ plus the law when it suited him but denied the benefits of the law to others who heard him. He had also apparently argued with the great apostle Peter.

Paul begins by setting the record straight. His conversion is well attested, as is the consistency of his message. Furthermore, he got this by direct revelation from the risen Christ. When he did eventually visit Jerusalem the church leaders confirmed that he preached the same message of salvation by faith alone as they did. They recognised his calling to the Gentiles and blessed his ministry.

The confrontation with Peter in Antioch was more important. Peter had compromised fellowship with Gentile believers. Apart from his actions being hurtful to his Christian brothers, it raised serious issues about the basis for salvation. Ethnic Jews who had become Christians had discovered that they could not be saved by keeping the Jewish law. They put their faith solely in Christ. Was Peter asking that Gentiles who had done the same should now adopt Jewish law and customs to be fully accepted? That would destroy the uniqueness of salvation by grace, says Paul.

Since the Jew was defined as a law-keeper over against Gentile sinners, does not this message of faith alone put Jewish Christians on a par with Gentile sinners? Surely this would make Christ a sin promoter? No way, says Paul. However, if we restore the law to our lives, which we know we can't keep, then we will redefine ourselves as lawbreakers, just like Gentile sinners.

So what becomes of the law? It's no longer relevant. We died with Christ; we rose with Christ. Our old life is over. We are neither Gentile sinners nor Jewish legalists. Christ, the faithful One, lives in us and He is the driving force in our lives. Basing our acceptance with God on anything else makes the work of Christ worthless.

Use the Discussion Starters to ensure that your group have followed the arguments. Discussion Starter 1 gives you the opportunity to stress that although Paul's humanity shines through his writings, that is a merit not a demerit. Paul writes God's truth under the anointing of the Holy Spirit. Discussion Starters 2 and 3 allow your group to summarise and explain Christ's Person and work. Use Discussion Starters 4 and 5 to emphasise that salvation can never be by works of our own doing.

You should read the Personal Application in order to address Discussion Starter 6 and the importance of equal fellowship among believers of differing backgrounds.

Read the Seeing Jesus section to answer Discussion Starter 7. Stress that our new life in Christ is about Him living His life of grace through us. It is very different from living by rules!

Week 3: The Law and the Promise

Opening Icebreaker

This session is very much about the gift of the promised Holy Spirit. Encourage your group to give brief testimonies of what the Holy Spirit has been doing in their lives. The correct answer to the question about our contribution is, of course, nothing – apart from faith.

Aim of the Session

We cannot overestimate the importance of receiving the gift of the Holy Spirit. It is the Spirit who confirms that we are the children of God and are therefore justified by faith. This was certainly the experience of the Galatian believers; indeed, their charismatic experience included many miracles in the bargain.

All this was now under threat; another spirit was at work

among them, one that would deceive them into imagining that having started in the Spirit they could now continue their spiritual journey only by depending upon their own efforts. The Galatians has foolishly fallen for a patent lie.

To prove his point Paul takes his readers back to the agreed fountainhead of the Jewish people. Abraham was justified by faith; he was a believer who never supposed for one moment that he could make himself right with God by his own efforts. Furthermore, God promised Abraham that all the nations, i.e. the Gentiles, would be blessed through him. Abraham's faith in Christ is all that is required to become children of Abraham.

In stark contrast, those who depend upon law-works are cursed with the impossibility of ever getting it right. There is also no compatibility between law-works and faith, between doing and believing. If we decide to save ourselves then Christ cannot save us. And we cannot save ourselves.

What Christ did was to bear the curse of the law on Himself, thereby freeing us from any liability or obligation to the law. He made this sacrifice so that we might receive the Holy Spirit.

Should we be in any doubt, remember this is an unbreakable covenant promise made by God Himself. The law cannot annul this promise which was earlier made to Abraham and to his Seed, who is Christ Himself. All who by faith put themselves in Christ become automatic beneficiaries of that promise.

Discussion Starter 1 invites us to consider works based religions such as Islam, Hinduism and Judaism, along with New Age religions and other cults such as Jehovah's Witnesses. Help your group see that the Christian faith doesn't fit normal religious categories.

Discussion Starters 2 and 3 focus our attention on the promise of the Holy Spirit. There is no technique for receiving the Spirit; all it requires is the openness and trust of humble faith.

Discussion Starters 4, 5 and 6 enable us to discuss the futility of self-righteousness and the impossibility of saving ourselves. If God is righteous and holy then how can sinners stand before Him? We have all fallen short of His glory. Jesus willingly took this curse upon Himself. If faith saves us then faith must keep us. Our sins need confessing and cleansing through the cross of Christ; there is nothing else that we can or should do. Read the Personal Application section at this point. Help your group realise how great it is to live by the Holy Spirit rather than being trapped on the seesaw of blessing and cursing.

To address Discussion Starter 7 read the Seeing Jesus section. This reminds us that our earthly history is intimately tied up with the parallel universe of the heavenly places. Jesus is the promised Seed and He has won the long battle with Satan. All those who take refuge in Him become part of that victorious Seed.

Week 4: The Slaves and the Sons

Opening Icebreaker

Prior to the meeting you will need to create several written charters personalised for each member of your group. Having distributed these, meditate for a few minutes, then ask your group members what their charter means to them.

Aim of the Session

Following the Bible readings, get your group to read the key verse aloud to one another. The United Kingdom does not have a formal constitution, holy book or legal code to which everyone agrees. This makes it harder for us to understand the ancient Jewish mindset. For them the Mosaic Law had the absolute authority of a police state backed by God Himself. Paul's teaching appeared to be an invitation to anarchy.

Paul affirms that the law is good but rejects the idea that it could ever grant eternal life. The law served a temporary purpose; it was to define precisely what constituted sin. It was never intended to be a pathway to salvation. Nor could it be, for we are all captives to sin, trapped in a cycle of human effort and failure overshadowed by the impossible demands of the law.

The law had another purpose: it was to educate us into the meaning of righteousness and to point us to the coming Righteous One. The advent of Christ, the promised Seed, heralded a new age where righteousness would be granted to us through faith. Having obtained this righteousness, we no longer need the law's supervision, nor its old divisive categories. We become one new man in Christ. After centuries of slavishly learning the rules, we may at last grow up. Jesus, the Son of God and the Son of Man paid the ultimate price to make this possible, and the Holy Spirit inspires our hearts to address God maturely as our intimate Father.

Discussion Starter 1 will help us clarify the purpose of the law and the reasons why it is now redundant once we put our faith in Christ. Some may think this a very risky position to hold. Use Discussion Starter 2 to emphasise the transforming power of the life, death and resurrection that we undergo when we are baptised into Christ. Using

Discussion Starter 3, check that people understand the radical change that took place in their hearts when they believed.

Devout Jews still wait for the coming of their Messiah. In approaching Discussion Starter 4 you need to show from the prophetic scriptures that Jesus fulfils all the messianic promises. See how many you know! Read the Seeing Jesus section at this point and note that Jesus came at the best of times, and the worst of times, but He came in God's time.

Ritualistic cults and religions keep people spiritually immature. God's will is that we grow up into Christ. Instead of slavishly serving the creation we become heirs to creation. Discussion Starter 5 is designed to help us consider how we approach those who are still immature slaves to the elemental spirits of the world.

Every believer needs consciously to experience the sealing of the Spirit, otherwise they will not be assured of their salvation. Check this out with Discussion Starter 6. You might want to pray for some who lack this assurance.

Read the Personal Application section and then address Discussion Starter 7. Many in our society have been deeply hurt by the attitudes of churchgoers, so much so that some hate the Church. We need to do better! Our unity in Christ cannot be merely a theological statement; it must be modelled before a watching world. Encourage the group to examine their hearts and lives to see if they are living in good fellowship with others. If some are willing to share any difficulties they may be experiencing, pray for them together.

Week 5: The Slave Woman and the Free Woman

Opening Icebreaker

Some members of your group may have come from
ethnic backgrounds where cultural and religious gods
were literally idols that held them in bondage. Others may
have been bound by ritualistic versions of Christianity.
For yet others their dependency gods might consist of
superstitious habits or ritual compulsions or addictive
behaviour.

Aim of the Session

For the apostle Paul, in the light of Christ's incarnation,
adherence to the law represented an immature religious
development. Making more rules and regulations might
seem like progress but it is actually a retrograde step.
In fact, those who do so are just as superstitious as the
pagans, vainly hoping that their rituals will somehow
compensate for their inability to keep the law. They have
sold themselves into demonic bondage in an effort to
salve their guilty consciences and retain their pride. Use
Discussion Starters 1 and 2 to explore how we can help
both the superstitious person and the religiously ritualistic
person find true freedom in Christ.

Paul's personal grief is evident. His readers had received
him as Christ's messenger. They had entered into a
personal relationship with God, but now they are in
danger of throwing it all away. Discussion Starter 3 invites
us to talk about the wonder and importance of that
personal relationship in the face of those who say it is
vain to make that claim when we are specks of dust in a
vast universe. Inventing codes of conduct seems more real!

Do Paul's concerns about religious feasts mean that we
should not celebrate Christmas or Easter? Some have

thought so. Emphasise that there is a difference between a celebration and an obligation. Giving thanks for the goodness of God is one thing; fearing divine judgment if we don't keep the day is quite another. Explore this using Discussion Starter 4.

To expose the truth about Jew-makers, Paul draws an analogy between Abraham's two sons, Ishmael and Isaac, and two covenants. It's a clever device; the Jew-makers respected Abraham and knew that Ishmael was rejected in favour of Isaac. Boldly, Paul places them and their teaching in the line of despised Ishmael. Indeed, he goes so far as to identify the covenant of law with the bond slave, Hagar, because the conception of her son was not of faith. In doing so, he has categorised both the Arabs and Jews as being in the same bondage! Use Discussion Starter 5 to help your group understand the meaning of this analogy.

Faith, on the other hand, anticipates the heavenly Jerusalem. When Moses built the tabernacle in the wilderness (on which the later Temple was based), he was instructed to follow a heavenly template. This was so that the earthly model would direct people's minds to the heavenly mother Jerusalem who, through Mary, would give birth to the true Descendant of Abraham and Sarah. Read the Seeing Jesus section and use Discussion Starter 6 to draw out the contrasts between the earthly city of legalistic religion and the heavenly city of grace and faith. Recognise, nonetheless, that the Temple design and worship all points to the coming of Christ and His sacrifice on our behalf.

Read the Personal Application section. Throughout Scripture Satan has fought against the coming of the Seed. One manifestation of that conflict was Ishmael's persecution of Isaac. There is no compatibility between bondage to law and faith in the promise. Use Discussion

Starter 7 to discuss the reasons for this conflict. Think about the arrogance and exclusivity that the law produces, and the vested interests of politics, business and religion that are so alien to the Spirit of Christ.

Week 6: Liberty and Love

Opening Icebreaker

It is always easy to find fault with God's people. This Icebreaker is an opportunity for us to talk about the love that we receive within the Christian community. It should be an opportunity for thanksgiving rather than self-congratulation!

Aim of the Session

In this session we come to the practical heart of Paul's argument. What is it that defines and identifies these people who call themselves Christians? It is an entirely new way of living. They are neither religious rule-keepers, nor licentious pagans. Instead, they demonstrate love for one another and for those around them. That love has its source and inspiration in Christ. He, through love, has fulfilled the law on our behalf and now enables us to do the same.

However, all this is negated if we choose the route of law-works. Use Discussion Starter 1 to make the point that if we take the path of legalism we fall from grace. Beware of anyone who forces you so dangerously off track. Circumcision is a one-way ticket away from Christ. Those who take this route would become Jews, not Christians.

In reality, the covenant mark of circumcision is irrelevant to the gospel. Mutilating the body cannot improve the soul.

If it could, then people might as well castrate themselves entirely and be done with it! Only Christ can save the soul and transform our lives. In the face of many religions and spiritual technologies, use Discussion Starter 2 to help members of your group express why they don't need anything else.

One criticism of justification by faith alone is that it might allow us to live lawlessly while claiming to have 'believed'. History has many examples to support this claim, such as imperially imposed baptism without a changed heart. Use Discussion Starter 3 to address the dangers of 'insurance policy' believe-ism. True faith will always express itself in transformed living; anything else is pure hypocrisy. Believers are free, but we are not free to do as we please. We have been set free from the power of the law, and from the power of sin. We are free to love. That is both the limit and the full extent of Christian freedom.

This is a powerful and positive truth. It can easily degenerate into a belief that decency is enough. Read the Personal Application section at this point then use Discussion Starter 4. The sins of the socially well-adjusted may be effectively hidden but they are still sins! Love is a positive action springing from a transformed heart. It is much more than social pleasantness.

Self-salvation always leads to competitiveness, elitism and pride. Christian communities that lose their dependency upon grace may easily become self-devouring. Churches do not die out without a cause, and that cause is most usually within. Use Discussion Starter 5 to address this serious issue. Are we becoming rule-bound? Are we using our longstanding position as a barrier to change? Discussion Starter 6 points to the antidote. If we use our freedom to love and serve one another then we fulfil God's law yet remain free from the curse of the law and its associated divisiveness.

Love expressed only within the family of God becomes incestuous unless we also serve those around us. Read the Seeing Jesus section then use Discussion Starter 7 to talk practically about how we engage in acts of practical love in the local community and beyond. Jesus sets the pattern for us by His 'doing and teaching' ministry. Think about how we can express our faith in the same manner in our daily lives.

Week 7: The Spirit and the Flesh

Opening Icebreaker

This is an opportunity to pray for one another's spiritual growth. There may be some who feel they must try harder. Encourage them that by walking in the Spirit the fruit will grow naturally.

Aim of the Session

There are two driving forces in our lives – the power of the flesh (NIV – the sinful nature) or the power of the Spirit. They are totally incompatible with one another. It is impossible to live according to the flesh and according to the Spirit at the same time. The way to overcome the cravings of the sinful nature is to live by the Spirit. It cannot be achieved by means of the Old Testament law. Indeed, to live by the law instead of trusting in Jesus is just another subtle way of serving the sinful nature.

In the same way, political idealism always fails because of human nature. Use Discussion Starter 1 to consider this. Maybe our politicians can do more to encourage those whose faith produces goodness rather than simply making more laws. However, it is not the job of politicians to change people's hearts. That is what the Church is for!

Use Discussion Starter 2 to reflect upon the sanctifying work of the Holy Spirit in our lives. Note how He releases us from bondage so that we are able to love people with Christ's love. Discussion Starter 3 presents a challenge. Are we living in such a manner that our non-Christian friends want to ask the question? There is something strangely relaxing about doing life this way; we simply allow the Holy Spirit to work through our surrendered selves.

In contrast to the destructive violence produced by the sinful nature, the Holy Spirit is a gardener. He grows fruit. Fruit is not there just to be admired; it is for nourishing others. Read the Personal Application section, using Discussion Starter 4 to understand what a virtuous life looks like. It is all about personal relationships, not just with those we love, but with everybody, even those who dislike us. Paul reminds us of our identification with Christ's crucifixion. Our Christian walk began with surrendering our will to the Holy Spirit. That is how it should continue.

Discussion Starter 5 invites us to examine these two driving forces – the sinful nature and the Holy Spirit. Emphasise the fundamental, non-negotiable law of sowing and reaping. Our Christian liberty grants us a choice of seed. We will reap precisely what we sow. Sowing to the sinful nature by legalistic self-righteousness or by serving destructive lusts is exhausting. Sowing to the Spirit may also take its toll, but what a difference in the harvest!

None of us gets it right all the time. Sometimes, we or others may sin badly. We must take responsibility for our own actions and humbly repent. It's no use blaming God or the devil. But what do we do about a brother or sister caught in sin? Use Discussion Starter 6 to address this question. We should be committed to restoration, recognising our own vulnerability, and doing what we can to help them back on their feet. Our job is not to destroy but to do good.

Read the Seeing Jesus section before tackling Discussion Starter 7. Paul concludes by going to the heart of the matter. The Jew-makers were proud cowards. They wanted self glory at the expense of the cross of Christ. This is the heart of false religion. Paul is finished with it. A new creation is emerging, a new Israel that has no part with the world's lawlessness, nor its religions. This new creation glories only in the cross of Christ.

National Distributors

UK: (and countries not listed below)
CWR, Waverley Abbey House, Waverley Lane, Farnham, Surrey GU9 8EP.
Tel: (01252) 784700 Outside UK (44) 1252 784700 Email: mail@cwr.org.uk

AUSTRALIA: KI Entertainment, Unit 21 317-321 Woodpark Road, Smithfield, New South Wales 2164. Tel: 1 800 850 777 Fax: 02 9604 3699 Email: sales@kientertainment.com.au

CANADA: David C Cook Distribution Canada, PO Box 98, 55 Woodslee Avenue, Paris, Ontario N3L 3E5. Tel: 1800 263 2664 Email: sandi.swanson@davidccook.ca

GHANA: Challenge Enterprises of Ghana, PO Box 5723, Accra. Tel: (021) 222437/223249 Fax: (021) 226227 Email: ceg@africaonline.com.gh

HONG KONG: Cross Communications Ltd, 1/F, 562A Nathan Road, Kowloon.
Tel: 2780 1188 Fax: 2770 6229 Email: cross@crosshk.com

INDIA: Crystal Communications, 10-3-18/4/1, East Marredpalli, Secunderabad – 500026, Andhra Pradesh. Tel/Fax: (040) 27737145 Email: crystal_edwj@rediffmail.com

KENYA: Keswick Books and Gifts Ltd, PO Box 10242-00400, Nairobi.
Tel: (254) 20 312639/3870125 Email: keswick@swiftkenya.com

MALAYSIA: Canaanland, No. 25 Jalan PJU 1A/41B, NZX Commercial Centre, Ara Jaya, 47301 Petaling Jaya, Selangor. Tel: (03) 7885 0540/1/2 Fax: (03) 7885 0545 Email: info@canaanland.com.my

Salvation Publishing & Distribution Sdn Bhd, 23 Jalan SS 2/64, 47300 Petaling Jaya, Selangor.
Tel: (03) 78766411/78766797 Fax: (03) 78757066/78756360
Email: info@salvationbookcentre.com

NEW ZEALAND: KI Entertainment, Unit 21 317-321 Woodpark Road, Smithfield,
New South Wales 2164, Australia. Tel: 0 800 850 777 Fax: +612 9604 3699
Email: sales@kientertainment.com.au

NIGERIA: FBFM, Helen Baugh House, 96 St Finbarr's College Road, Akoka, Lagos.
Tel: (01) 7747429/4700218/825775/827264 Email: fbfm_1@yahoo.com

PHILIPPINES: OMF Literature Inc, 776 Boni Avenue, Mandaluyong City.
Tel: (02) 531 2183 Fax: (02) 531 1960 Email: gloadlaon@omflit.com

SINGAPORE: Alby Commercial Enterprises Pte Ltd, 95 Kallang Avenue #04-00, AIS Industrial Building, 339420. Tel: (65) 629 27238 Fax: (65) 629 27235 Email: marketing@alby.com.sg

SOUTH AFRICA: Struik Christian Books, 80 MacKenzie Street, PO Box 1144, Cape Town 8000.
Tel: (021) 462 4360 Fax: (021) 461 3612 Email: info@struikchristianmedia.co.za

SRI LANKA: Christombu Publications (Pvt) Ltd, Bartleet House, 65 Braybrooke Place, Colombo 2.
Tel: (9411) 2421073/2447665 Email: dhanad@bartleet.com

USA: David C Cook Distribution Canada, PO Box 98, 55 Woodslee Avenue, Paris, Ontario N3L 3E5, Canada. Tel: 1800 263 2664 Email: sandi.swanson@davidccook.ca

Courses and seminars

Publishing and new media

Conference facilities

Transforming lives

CWR's vision is to enable people to experience personal transformation through applying God's Word to their lives and relationships.

Our Bible-based training and resources help people around the world to:
- Grow in their walk with God
- Understand and apply Scripture to their lives
- Resource themselves and their church
- Develop pastoral care and counselling skills
- Train for leadership
- Strengthen relationships, marriage and family life

and much more.

Our insightful writers provide daily Bible-reading notes and other resources for all ages, and our experienced course designers and presenters have gained an international reputation for excellence and effectiveness.

CWR's Training and Conference Centre in Surrey, England, provides excellent facilities in an idyllic setting – ideal for both learning and spiritual refreshment.

CWR Applying God's Word
to everyday life and relationships

CWR, Waverley Abbey House,
Waverley Lane, Farnham,
Surrey GU9 8EP, UK

Telephone: **+44 (0)1252 784700**
Email: **info@cwr.org.uk**
Website: **www.cwr.org.uk**

Registered Charity No 294387
Company Registration No 1990308

Dramatic new resource

Prayers of Jesus - Hearing His heartbeat
by Peter Hicks

Take a closer look at Jesus' prayers gain insight from the context of Jesus' prayers, enjoy a more intimate relationship with the Father and consider why Jesus *didn't* pray for some things.

72-page booklet, 148x210mm
ISBN: 978-1-85345-647-3

The bestselling *Cover to Cover* Bible Study Series

1 Corinthians
Restoring harmony
ISBN: 978-1-85345-374-8

2 Corinthians
Growing a Spirit-filled church
ISBN: 978-1-85345-551-3

1 Timothy
Healthy churches –
effective Christians
ISBN: 978-1-85345-291-8

23rd Psalm
The Lord is my shepherd
ISBN: 978-1-85345-449-3

2 Timothy and Titus
Vital Christianity
ISBN: 978-1-85345-338-0

Acts 1-12
Church on the move
ISBN: 978-1-85345-574-2

Acts 13-28
To the ends of the earth
ISBN: 978-1-85345-592-6

Ecclesiastes
Hard questions and
spiritual answers
ISBN: 978-1-85345-371-7

Elijah
A man and his God
ISBN: 978-1-85345-575-9

Ephesians
Claiming your inheritance
ISBN: 978-1-85345-229-1

Esther
For such a time as this
ISBN: 978-1-85345-511-7

Fruit of the Spirit
Growing more like Jesus
ISBN: 978-1-85345-375-5

Galatians
Freedom in Christ
ISBN: 978-1-85345-648-0

Genesis 1-11
Foundations of reality
ISBN: 978-1-85345-404-2

God's Rescue Plan
Finding God's fingerprints
on human history
ISBN: 978-1-85345-294-9

Great Prayers of the Bible
Applying them to our lives today
ISBN: 978-1-85345-253-6

Hebrews
Jesus – simply the best
ISBN: 978-1-85345-337-3

Hosea
The love that never fails
ISBN: 978-1-85345-290-1

Isaiah 1-39
Prophet to the nations
ISBN: 978-1-85345-510-0

Isaiah 40-66
Prophet of restoration
ISBN: 978-1-85345-550-6

James
Faith in action
ISBN: 978-1-85345-293-2

For current prices or to order visit www.cwr.org.uk/store
Available online or from Christian bookshops.

Cover to Cover Every Day
Gain deeper knowledge of the Bible

Each issue of these bimonthly daily Bible-reading notes gives you insightful commentary on a book of the Old and New Testaments with reflections on a psalm each weekend by Philip Greenslade.

Enjoy contributions from two well-known authors every two months, and over a five-year period you will be taken through the entire Bible.

Only £2.85 each (plus p&p)
£15.50 for UK annual subscription (bimonthly, p&p included)
£13.80 for annual email subscription
(available from www.cwr.org.uk/store)

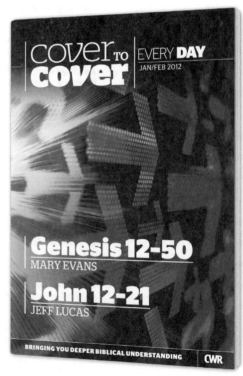

Cover to Cover Complete
Read through the Bible chronologically

Take an exciting, year-long journey through the Bible, following events as they happened.

- See God's strategic plan of redemption unfold across the centuries
- Increase your confidence in the Bible as God's inspired message
- Come to know your heavenly Father in a deeper way

The full text of the flowing Holman Christian Standard Bible (HCSB) provides an exhilarating reading experience and is augmented by our beautiful:

- Illustrations
- Maps
- Charts
- Diagrams
- Timeline

And key Scripture verses and devotional thoughts make each day's reading more meaningful.

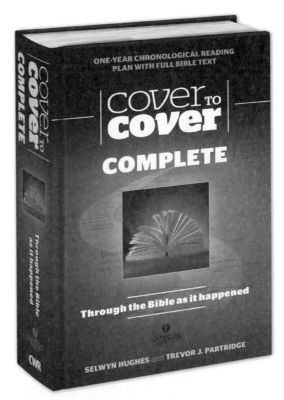